# Principles of Macroeconomics

## READINGS, ISSUES, AND CASES

*Second Edition*

*A companion volume by Edwin Mansfield*

Principles of Macroeconomics, *Second Edition*

# Principles of Macroeconomics

READINGS, ISSUES, AND CASES

*Second Edition*

Edited by
# EDWIN MANSFIELD
UNIVERSITY OF PENNSYLVANIA

W·W· NORTON & COMPANY · INC · NEW YORK

ISBN 0 393 09108 2

Printed in the United States of America

2 3 4 5 6 7 8 9 0

**Acknowledgments**

Permission to use copyrighted materials from the following sources is hereby acknowledged.

"Is Economics Obsolete? No, Underemployed" by Charles L. Schultze. Copyright 1972 by Saturday Review Co. First appeared in *Saturday Review,* January 22, 1972. Used with permission of the publisher and the author. "The Price System" by W. Allen Wallis. Reprinted by permission from *The Freeman,* July 1957. "The Economic Organisation of a P.O.W. Camp" by R. A. Radford from *Economica,* November 1945. Used with permission of the publisher. "Capitalism: An Irrational System" by Paul Baran and Paul Sweezy. Copyright © 1966 by Paul M. Sweezy; reprinted by permission of Monthly Review Press. "The Future of Capitalism" by Robert L. Heilbroner from *Business Civilization in Decline,* pp. 17–34. By permission of W. W. Norton & Company, Inc. © W. W. Norton & Company, Inc. "The Government of the Economy" by George J. Stigler in *A Dialogue on the Proper Economic Role of the State,* 1963 (Selected Papers No. 7, The Graduate School of Business). Reprinted by permission of The Graduate School of Business (University of Chicago). "The Economic Role of Private Activity" by Paul A. Samuelson from *A Dialogue on the Proper Economic Role of the State.* Reprinted by permission of the Graduate School of Business (University of Chicago) and by the author. "The Great Depression," reprinted from the September 1932 issue of *Fortune* magazine by special permission; © 1932 Time Inc. "Fiscal Policy and Economic Stabilization" from *Federal Tax Policy* by Joseph A. Pechman. © 1971 by the Brookings Institution. Reprinted by permission of the Brookings Institution. "Fiscal Policy—A Skeptical View" by Milton Friedman from *Capitalism and Freedom,* originally published in 1962. Reprinted by permission of The University of Chicago Press and the author. "The Need for Federal Balanced Budgets" by Maurice H. Stans (Director of the Budget 1958–61). © The American Academy of Political and Social Science. Reprinted by permission of the publisher and author. "Deficit, Deficit, Who's Got the Deficit?" Reprinted by permission from *National Economic Policy* by James Tobin. Copyright © 1966 by Yale University. "Economic Forecasting and Sciences" by Paul A. Samuelson. Reprinted by permission of the publisher, The University of Michigan, © 1965. "Is Monetary Policy Being Oversold?" Reprinted from *Monetary vs. Fiscal Policy* by Milton Friedman and Walter Heller. By permission of W. W. Norton & Company, Inc. © 1969 by The Graduate School of Business Administration, New York University. "Has Fiscal Policy Been Oversold?" Reprinted from *Monetary vs. Fiscal Policy* by Milton Friedman and Walter W. Heller. By permission of W. W. Norton & Company, Inc. © 1969 by The Graduate School of Business Administration, New York University. "Rules and Roles for Fiscal and Monetary Policy" by Arthur M. Okun from *Issues in Fiscal and Monetary Policy: The Eclectic Economist Views the Controversy,* published by the DePaul University Press. Reprinted by permission of the author and the publisher. "Makers of Monetary Policy." Reprinted from *Managing the Dollar* by Sherman J. Maisel. By permission of W. W. Norton & Company, Inc. © 1973 by Sherman J. Maisel. "Open-Market Operations: A Case Study." Reprinted by permission of Paul Meek, Monetary Adviser, from *Open-Market Operations,* published and copyrighted by the Federal Reserve Bank of New York, 1973. "The Fed in a Political World" by David P. Eastman from *Business Review,* October, 1975. Reprinted by permission of the author. © Federal Reserve Bank of Philadelphia. "The Intelligent Citizen's Guide to Inflation" by Robert M. Solow. Reprinted by permission of the author from *The Public Interest,* No. 38, Winter 1975. © 1975 by National Affairs, Inc. "The Inflationary Bias in Our Economy" by Arthur F. Burns. Reprinted by permission of the author from his address, "The Real Issues of Inflation and Unemployment," delivered at the University of Georgia, September 19, 1975. "What Have We Learned about Inflation?" by Henry C. and Mable I. Wallich from *Challenge,* published by International Arts and Sciences Press, Inc., White Plains, New York 10603. Reprinted by permission of the publisher. "What Price Guideposts?" by Milton Friedman in G. Shultz and R. Aliber, *Guidelines: Informal Controls and the Marketplace,* 1966, published by The University of Chicago Press. Reprinted by permission of the author and the publisher. "The Case against the Case against the Guideposts" by Robert Solow in G. Shultz and R. Aliber, *Guidelines: Informal Controls and the Marketplace,* 1962. Reprinted by permission of the author and the publisher. "The Case against Economic Growth" from *The Costs of Economic Growth* by E. J. Mishan. Reprinted by permission of Praeger Publishers, Inc. "The Limits to Growth" from *The Limits to Growth* by Donella H. Meadows, Dennis L. Meadows, Jorgen Randers, William W. Behrens III, a Potomac Associates book, published by Universe Books, New York, 1972. "Is the End of the World at Hand?" by Robert M. Solow. Reprinted by permission from *Challenge,* published by International Arts and Sciences Press, Inc., White Plains, New York 10603. "Contribution of Research and Development to Economic Growth in the United States" by Edwin Mansfield, originally published in *Science,* Vol. 175, pp. 477–486, February 4, 1972. © 1972 by the American Association for the Advancement of Science. Reprinted by permission. "Economic Incentives in Air-Pollution Control." Reprinted from *The Economics of Air Pollution, A Symposium,* edited by Harold Wolozin. By permission of W. W. Norton & Company, Inc. © 1966 by W. W. Norton & Company, Inc. "The International Economic System and the Multinational Corporation" by Lawrence B. Krause. Reprinted by permission from *The International Economic System and the Multinational Corporation,* Volume 403, September 1972 issue, pp. 93–103, of *The Annals* of The American Academy of Political and Social Science. © The American Academy of Political and Social Science. "The Multinational Firm and Imperialism" from Paul A. Baran's *The Political Economy of Growth.* © 1957 by Monthly Review Inc., reprinted by permission of Monthly Review Press. "The New Protectionism" by Walter Adams. Originally published in *Challenge,* May-June 1973. Reprinted by permission of the publisher. "The Poor Nations." Reprinted from *The Rich Nations and the Poor Nations* by Barbara Ward. By permission of W. W. Norton & Company, Inc. © 1962 by Barbara Ward. "The Less Developed Countries: Observations and Implications." Reprinted from Simon Kuznets, *Population, Capital, and Growth.* By permission of W. W. Norton & Company, Inc. © 1973 by W. W. Norton & Co., Inc. "Economic Growth in the Developing Countries." Reprinted from *Economic Progress and Policy in Developing Countries* by Angus Maddison. By permission of W. W. Norton & Company, Inc. © 1970 by George Allen & Unwin, Ltd.